IMAGES
of America

EARLY-20TH-CENTURY
LOS ANGELES
BUNGALOW ARCHITECTURE

IMAGES
of America

EARLY-20TH-CENTURY
LOS ANGELES
BUNGALOW ARCHITECTURE

Harry Zeitlin and Bennett Gilbert

ARCADIA
PUBLISHING

Copyright © 2022 by Harry Zeitlin and Bennett Gilbert
ISBN 978-1-4671-0903-1

Published by Arcadia Publishing
Charleston, South Carolina

Printed in the United States of America

Library of Congress Control Number: 2022938572

For all general information, please contact Arcadia Publishing:
Telephone 843-853-2070
Fax 843-853-0044
E-mail sales@arcadiapublishing.com
For customer service and orders:
Toll-Free 1-888-313-2665

Visit us on the Internet at www.arcadiapublishing.com

CONTENTS

Acknowledgments

All the images in this book were photographed by Harry Zeitlin and appear courtesy of the authors, with the exception of the photograph on page 127. The introductions and commentary were written by Bennett Gilbert

Material help, great ideas, an education in photography, and friendly comfort made it possible for us to wander around the neighborhoods of Los Angeles, seeking bungalows and shooting these photographs. Our family members then living in Los Angeles, including Jake Zeitlin, David Zeitlin, and Stella Gilbert, taught us much that we needed to know and were frequent sources of assistance. Aaron Rapoport, Michael Sullivan, Rick Okie, and others from the diaspora of our college class helped out in this project as well.

But it was an assortment of acquaintances who made the days sweet for us: Armando Sarabia, who fed us well for almost no money at his restaurant on Western Avenue, the Gaucho Sarabia; the Capra family at their Italian market; the unheralded genius of ice cream, Karmin, of Karmin's Ice Cream on Third and Berendo Streets; Raul, who kept our squirrelly cars running; and Sarkis and Adonis, who never failed to find what we needed.

In these years, Isabel Holt and the other hosts of *Morning Becomes Electric* on KCRW and the DJs at KPFK were constant company for us both.

INTRODUCTION

"Nothing," wrote the aged Los Angeles newspaperman Murray Carr in 1935, "Nothing can now be done about the dreadful bungalows that litter the flatlands." Development would, in its inevitable way, bring less humble, though more dreadful, homes, generations of mansions cascading across the side lawns and fruit-tree yards of the bungalows, investors replacing citizens and some kind of proud capital that Carr fantasized in place of the simpler fantasy bungalows conjured. He would perhaps have been pleased, as well, that the 1960s and 1970s brought asbestos shingles and "texturized" spray-coated stucco to the little horrors, perhaps gleeful that dingbat apartment buildings—four apartments on top, four in the middle, cars on the bottom, named after the builder's daughters—with dwarf palms and multicolored Malibu flood lamps and crossed Tahitian spears have ingested the dreadful litter as the big fish swallows the smaller. Yet bigger fish swallowed the dingbats: five or six layers of apartments, perhaps flanking a cone-hatted tower above a row of shops. As each generation of ugly or bizarre buildings is demolished by its successor, there are indeed always those who believe Los Angeles is little that is not dreadful litter. Down at the lowest archaeo-architectural sediment, however, the bungalow remains, formerly forgotten, now sometimes treasured, polished, and replumbed, because after all, the best domestic architecture in the flatlands was and is the bungalow.

Because they are an essentially neighborhood architecture, bungalows are still found in great numbers in the oldest surviving and most characteristic communities of Los Angeles. For 100 or 120 years, they have been lived in as steadily and happily as most people can live. They bore the litter of half of that life as they ran to seed when we photographed them in 1976 and 1977. Many that survive unretouched now have twice the litter and adulteration. Yet they are the sort of building that dilapidates handsomely. Before they might all be torn down or tastelessly modernized, we decided to learn to look at them.

Before the many new museums, theaters, restaurants, and "retail experiences" of the last half-century, before round-the-clock shopping, and before armchair digital travel, it was a curious truth that the best entertainment in Los Angeles was to get in a car and drive around looking at the houses. This was an urban art, tied to finding small ethnic restaurants and neighborhoods when no public transport would conveniently take you to them. People in Los Angeles in those days were just beginning to realize that they might engage in the activities of hard-core big cities—that their own core had become hard, saturated, smelly, and lively. It was just when this kind of awareness led Los Angeles to think of itself as a great city that progress became a battle for its soul, just as it does in every great city. This entertainment of looking at the houses descended from the Sunday family diversion of piling into the car to look at new housing tracts. It depended upon envy and the desire to move upward. The first housing tracts in Southern California built for and visited by automobile—the engine itself of social as well as topographic mobility—were bungalows. Bungalows had been a means to provide housing for huge numbers of new arrivals that could help to settle them into industrial service by embedding

7

them in a myth of carefree life, a myth replaced in the 1930s by the myth of Hollywood glamor and then by other illusions.

But the photographer and author of this book did not have domesticated interests. Our desires were aesthetic and to a degree moral—to find beauty that was overlooked and slipped into desuetude. We set out to picture it. In doing so, we saw what people had stopped seeing around 1930. These photographs are now the sole documentation of many bungalow houses that have been demolished or altered beyond recognition.

The bungalows dominated home building in the region, with nationwide influence, from around 1900 to around 1930. The mid-1920s were their most prolific period. The picture of affordable comfort and available domestic safety that manifested the bungalow was stopped by a far richer and more deluxe imaginarium of commodified desire (among other forces): the architectural spectacles of Hollywood films, prolifically ballooning as the film industry waxed on the increasingly rare nickels and dimes of Americans seeking diversion from the Depression. The movies presented houses of every style; they could be made on studio lots and were built by developers across the Los Angeles basin and adjacent valleys for those whose visions of home, safety, and comfort the film industry had trained. Set decoration for Hollywood movies created complex, fragmented facades that entertained fantasies far greater than that of cozy comfort in the dark wood interiors of brown bungalows. In the 1930s, the bungalow quickly started to feel musty, old-fashioned, clumsy, crude, and poor. To live in a bungalow in the 1950s and 1960s was largely to live with the working class in old and rundown inner-city neighborhoods.

The result was that no one looked at the bungalow for its strengths for a long time until the authors did so in 1976 and 1977. When David Winter wrote the first published appreciation of bungalows, *The California Bungalow* of 1980, he observed that he could not find good photographs of bungalows and instead had to use the pictures that builders put into their old plan books from which aspiring homeowners chose the type of bungalow they wanted and could afford. He added, "There are literally no previous books on the bungalow." Apart from two articles by Anthony King in the *American Architectural Quarterly* in 1973, there was no retrospective study at all. The present book is, in fact, the very first renewed look at urban bungalow houses as a work of art and a part of life in Los Angeles ever made, although in the 45 years it has awaited publication other important books have given well-preserved bungalows a second life as homes and works of architectural art. A vast wave of interest in Los Angeles architecture has followed ever since 1980.

To our eyes today, the photographs of bungalows that Winter found in the books of plans for sale, such as those of the Los Angeles Investment Company, the De Luxe Building Company, and the M.S. Yeager and E.W. Stillwell companies as well as national retailers Sears & Roebuck and Montgomery Ward, do more to make the bungalow strange than they do to make it attractive. The bungalows look like farmhouses scattered on the prairie or like facades on a movie set before the rest of the scenery is brought. This both underlines and elides a part of their actuality. They were in fact a concept for the suburbs: houses, not city apartments, on tracts being developed outside the downtown cores in many cities, made possible by suburban (or "interurban") commuter rail transport lines and roads for automobiles. And so they were new on the land, yet to be coddled by grown trees and flowery gardens. This bareness suggested the freedom of the new break in life for the buyers. These houses were, nonetheless, destined to become urban, as creating or joining a city was the goal of every tract subdivision. The homeowner bought a bit of suburban heaven, at the same time building up the forces of urbanization that were to urbanize it, and also entering the multigenerational Ponzi scheme of profiting from home sales that were to make housing the most expensive product any citizen could want. The development companies used a narrow grey scale in these photographs and cheap reproduction technologies that washed out both the physical and social reality of the bungalow.

The photographs were part of the picture the verbal language of the plan books created. These sales pitches manipulated customers with a certain naivete and commonsensical pose that led buyers to think of the developer as their friendly partner in an enterprise for their mutual benefit. The developers stressed the family values of their houses, their willingness to accommodate the buyer's needs, the intimacy of the simple home, the rationality of prefabricated building methods, the attractive milieu of community, the sense of accomplishment the new homeowner would have in building the house, and the warm interest of the company in family well-being. Creating a new little world for the family on the good earth with such a partner for only $2,000 was irresistible. They were creating aesthetically appealing homes for an automobile-driving, mortgage-indebted middle-class that was being stuffed into the Los Angeles basin at unprecedented speed.

The business machinery behind the "Kozy Komfort" of the bungalow (as one advertisement put it) was less edifying but also very clever. It succeeded in combining together rejection of the box-shaped and boxed-off rooms of previous architecture with the trend of *Japonisme* (begun primarily in France and America at the end of the 19th century), Art and Crafts movement aesthetic and ethical ideals, the image of informal harmony with nature, modern hygienic conveniences, and traditional American territorial possessiveness. The mash-up of these trends, fancies, and pitches served to elevate the self-regard of the first-time home buyer, but it also served to make adventurous developers into a civic force. A good example is Henry L. Wilson, who called himself "the Bungalow Man" and published a popular journal about bungalows. He was both a monomaniac and flimflam artist, whose product promotion through magazines and his own identity gave him a career building bungalows in Los Angeles and Seattle. People like Wilson as well as their customers enabled the suburbanization fanning out from downtown.

A better example is the Los Angeles Investment Company. It was started by penniless musicians who could not find gigs. They developed a model of a cooperative building society, which eventually offered a bewildering array of shares, "Gold Notes," reinvestments, dividends, and discounts that appeared to pay returns upwards of 30 percent. The company built a large headquarters in downtown Los Angeles and started a bank. It was, of course, too good to be true: the owners went to prison for fraud, and the company was quietly rescued and dissolved by the banks that had become intertwined with it in order to avoid a collapse in real market values such as the bust after a boom had caused in 1887. They did not make whole the many little investors whose 25¢ deposits had seemed to accumulate into a house of their own or a secure rentier income. Real estate speculation had become a leading enterprise in Southern California by the late 1880s in consequence of the breakup of the vast rancho of Abel Stearns, who died in 1869, as the population increased 20 times over. The bungalow builders merely continued it, and they had many worthy successors in the period after World War II, from C.C. Fitzpatrick, who also went to federal prison, to the Janss Company, Nate Shappell, Mark Taper, Eli Broad, and the many other great banker and builder moguls of housing tract development throughout Southern California. The original and the greatest of all of course was the infamous swindle of Owens Valley water through the Los Angeles Aqueduct in 1905. The bungalow developer and buyer on the one hand and the streetcar line owners, automobile and gasoline industries, land developers, and banks on the other all depended on each other to create a world of American home ownership in the last half of the 20th century.

The Owens Valley water affair was the foundation for much of the development of the Los Angeles area, both as a real estate project and as a culture. The fact that the makers of the movie *Chinatown* (directed by Roman Polanski) in 1974 found enough of bungalow-era Los Angeles intact so as to be able to film it on the city streets signals the persistence of this basis in the Los Angeles that came to be. And the 1970s launched Los Angeles into its next era of megacity, with the problems of conurbation found around the world. At that moment a magic brought together in Los Angeles the artists and the culture, building on the scattered bohemia of postwar Southern California and then the beatnik and counter cultures, and made it a unique center of American life in the late 1970s. But soon it became as complex and troubled as the rest of the world—or, more precisely, before it ceased to be able to hide its troubles: the troubles of industrial society, of cities conjured by developed out of waterless deserts, of merciless marketing and endless exploitation of labor and resources, under the images of carefree and healthy life in a supposedly perfect and verdant climate. For a few years, the critique of America launched in the 1960s was leavened by the optimism of California in the smoggy valleys of Los Angeles, between its crazy patchwork downtown, the neighborhoods from Silverlake to Santa Monica just beginning to come back to life, to the Venice that seemed immortally uninhibited, bohemian, rundown, and cheap.

Venice, like Los Angeles, is now a mess of a kind Harry Carr could not have imagined. Economic warfare or "shock therapy" has assaulted the nation and the world in the last three decades, with its financialization of everything, control of the production and distribution of goods and services by people without the least whisper of interest in the skills of honest production and fair distribution, with its lawless galaxy of shell companies and real estate investment trusts for vast criminal or otherwise socially amoral fortunes, and a morally nearly mute public square. All this has left Los Angeles choked and crowded, though culturally and material richer than anyone in 1900 ever imagined it could be. The smog our camera tried to pierce is mostly gone, but the clearer air reveals the losses. In 1976, it was still a city of small old shops in the shadows of the new skyscrapers. It was freer than now, as was the national culture in which, in the 1960s and its wake, it was possible to live cheaply enough to experiment with living without working too hard. Because of that, we two, who were nearly penniless, had the time and the curiosity to try to see that city in 1976, still rather vulgar but also still good-hearted, as a home in which ordinary working people could buy a bit of beauty, even though the foundations of a new order were being prepared beneath their feet. The look of America in the 1970s was rather decayed, crummy, and badly appointed and designed. But something remained that now has been left behind. May these photographs glorify that hour.

One

THE BUNGALOW DREAM

It was a constant claim of the bungalow movement that it would build towns that were not like the crowded and dirty cities where one must live up the stairs or elevator, away from the good earth amid crowds and dirt. And it did produce a kind of home that was habitable, pretty, and indigenous to Southern California. No kind of building—not even the Spanish style—has given so much to the texture of the city because somehow its eccentricity gave to Los Angeles its former sense of infinite possibilities. That sense was the product of real estate salesmanship. But even as that faded, as the bungalow dilapidated gracefully, it still afforded good cheap housing in the 1970s until either demolition or restoration touched each bungalow home.

Its look created this feeling of open possibilities. Each on its own and together with its neighbors, its lines converge, contrast, and overlap. The lines do not move in the rhythms of earlier architecture. The eye has nowhere to rest. For a bungalow, there is no one most advantageous point of view, no dominant aspect or permanent image.

Because its appearance cannot be exhausted from any one point of view, the bungalow is an apt subject for the architectural photographer. The photographer can change his eye's entire system of perspective by taking a step or two to one side or the other, changing the camera's lens, or casting a new grid of perspectival lines over the subject. Thus, the bungalow suits the modern eye. As a species of good modern architecture, it breaks up perspective and axial alignment. It was the old Neoclassical and Victorian house box unfolded, exploding outward. Space and mass are irregular and subtle; from the outside, these are often open and flowing along horizontal lines.

These qualities inspired this photo essay.

849 North Mariposa Avenue, Hollywood. The house is intact but now somewhat overwhelmed by a large additional structure behind it. Here, the beams and joists of an extended open truss entry porch, supported by bevel-edged wood blocks on brick piers, create deep shade to project a strong and attractive entrance. The variegated textures give the simple house an air of luxury. The photograph of whitewash contrasted with the dark wood surfaces common to the bungalow shows both the solidity and airiness of the external parts of the house. As the orientation of the house number toward the street shows, the length of the porch is at a right angle to the street, pulling the occupant or visitor into domesticity by a walk in the shade.

6067 HAROLD WAY, HOLLYWOOD. The small house is intact and restored. A second-story gable canted forward emphasizes the horizontality of the ground floor at a right angle to it. Notably, the bay window also lengthens the living area but projects it into the private area at the side rather than toward the street frontage. Brick skirting and stone front steps support a long shallow front porch under a fringe of rafter tails. Bays reflect the frequent choice of small enclosed spaces in the interiors that balance the relatively open plan of living and dining rooms in many bungalows. This house is from the last wave of bungalow construction in the central Hollywood flatlands that finally supplanted most of the original scattered farmhouses and structures, building a residential community around Hollywood and Sunset Boulevards as commercial centers.

49 WAVECREST AVENUE, VENICE. This bungalow is now divided into apartments with a few improvements; the exterior is intact but unrestored. The viewer sees a high balcony supported by fanciful brackets under a broad gable, adjacent to a bay window. This house is on a Venice "walk street," where it was a part of the imagined community Abbot Kinney and others created as Venice, California, built on undervalued sandy land south of Santa Monica. At the time of this photograph, Venice had been deteriorating for decades; most of the canals were removed while those that remained were sludgy dumps. The whole area was, as Reyner Banham put it, "something between a ghetto and a hippie haven." It was, therefore, a cool place to live, a real beach village, set apart on its own with its back to the metropolis. Much of it has now become affluent.

4727 OAKWOOD AVENUE, HOLLYWOOD. Still intact, this house is in a common bungalow configuration—modest in scale but made to seem expansive by a deep porch wrapping around the front and side, further extended on the opposite side by a bay living room or dining room window with three sides echoed by a congruent roof. The double gable adds depth and completeness above, while the brick courses around both the porch and dining room emphasize horizontality. The lot is narrow, like many bungalow lots. This meant that it was difficult to enlarge the house, with the result that many owners eventually tore down bungalows to build up more lavish houses on accumulated land. The small front lawn here is the harbinger of this development.

1532 McCollum Street, Silver Lake (Above), and 1519–1521 East Sixtieth Street, Watts.
These two photographs illustrate opposite approaches to the gable features of the bungalow. The house in Silver Lake has impressive quadruple gables in an entertaining diamond pattern, with the bottom three symmetrically intersecting while the largest tops them all over three wide windows. The house sits on a slope in one of several serried shallow valleys in the older part of the neighborhood; the high lookout of the house seems to echo and respond to this as well, as to the slope of the street. Note the tiny porch and the intact original garage. The Watts house, on the other hand, is on flat topography and is one of the thousands of bungalows built for miles south of downtown. Here, one large tent-like gable sprouts one dormer facing the street and another capping the dining bay. Despite these differences, both retain something of the boxy verticality of the Queen Anne style that the bungalow supplanted. Both also are solidly working-class houses.

333 NORTH WILTON PLACE, HOLLYWOOD. Built in 1915, probably for less than $5,000, this house has been well preserved and is now a multimillion dollar property. The detail shown here is the lively open-truss front porch support. Although each element is strictly a functional support, the mechanism as a whole is hard to read and becomes instead a point of aesthetic interest, here accentuated in black and white. The main beams and rafters develop the pattern for a very large ground-floor gable covering a wide and impressive elevated porch landing.

990–998 ½ EVERETT STREET, ECHO PARK. In this house, the handsome wide gable roof has been replaced by a mansard, and the row of windows below it has been turned into a kind of glazed balcony. It was and is an apartment house. The development and regulation of apartments played a role in the history of the bungalow. A few were apartment houses, intended to match the standards the city then was developing for replacing tenements. The building is split-level, with stone-faced piers supporting the whole upper story and enclosing the kind of huge porch that was not uncommon in older apartment houses. Although the design is rigid, it is, nonetheless, the case that bungalow elements help the building define the street and the neighborhood.

2542 THIRD STREET, SANTA MONICA. The side of this house is more complex than the front. It is busier because there was more of the house's business to be done here: two square bays, back door, external staircase, and garage. In front, there is another bay window and a large upper-story bedroom dormer as well as a small gable for ventilation louvers. The external staircase and the small gable indicate a substantial landing between the two stories; bungalows often separated stairwells in various ways to minimize the space they required. The front gives a deceptively modest impression of the size of the house. Yet its size likely saved it, as it was big enough for postwar families or to serve as apartments. The building remains a large house, much better tended now than in 1976.

47 Wavecrest Avenue, Venice (above), and 714–716 South Irolo Street, Mid-Wilshire.
The lovely bungalow in Venice was designed for living by the shore, with lots of west-facing
windows and an upper-story sunroom. Its T-shape has beauty; the side gable is just the right size,
and the front gable is effortlessly integrated into it. Homes like this made Venice the image of an
ideal West Coast beach town. The house in central Los Angeles had the same kind of beauty—a
great sloping gable sets up the front porch and two second-floor bedrooms. Even the square window
on the left is eloquent. But note the decay and then the concrete building looming behind. The
concrete won—the house has been demolished.

209 SOUTH WILTON PLACE, MID-WILSHIRE. This intact house is part of a street of handsome large bungalows, all prosperous and contented. Yet this street- and neighborhood-size effect is built up out of details such as the one pictured here. On top of a pillar, two cut beams with rounded ends are joined mortice and tenon style, like fan blades. They connect the pillar and the huge main beam of the front porch, but they serve also to support the narrow gable that runs the length of the porch through a series of eccentrically articulated vertical and horizontal elements. Shingles complete the spreading eave. The rich assemblage of visually interesting intersections such as these helped to make each house in a row distinctive yet complementary.

CORNER OF LACRESTA COURT AND WESTERN AVENUE, HOLLYWOOD. LaCresta Court still stands, although some houses have been altered. This charming gatepost of clinker brink and arroyo rock, mixed in a motley manner, is topped by a cast concrete miniature bungalow cross-gabled roof with a little capstone. The whole object is an index of the notion of the bungalow as capable of creating community. In part, this idea was based on social and aesthetic ideals. But it was also a commercial concept, as the first bungalow courts were proto-motels for the family fleeing the harsh winter of colder climates. LaCresta Court is a community of single-family homes—many of which are not bungalows—on a street rather than a court, and the gatepost serves to display its street name, but it is also a compact symbol of the image of the bungalow in the city in the 1910s.

741 SOUTH IROLO STREET, MID-WILSHIRE. This fine house was designed by Alfred and Arthur Heineman, who constructed many bungalows in a distinctive style, and has been demolished and replaced with an apartment building. These details from the porch are typical of their work and are a study in the use of the upswept motif, or "pagoda," style. The rounded ends are reminiscent of the technique Greene and Greene made famous. Apart from the *Japonisme* air, what is notable is the legibility of structure. The lines are all strong, as only thick elements are used. They create a captivating sense of richness and intricacy. These photographs alone document it.

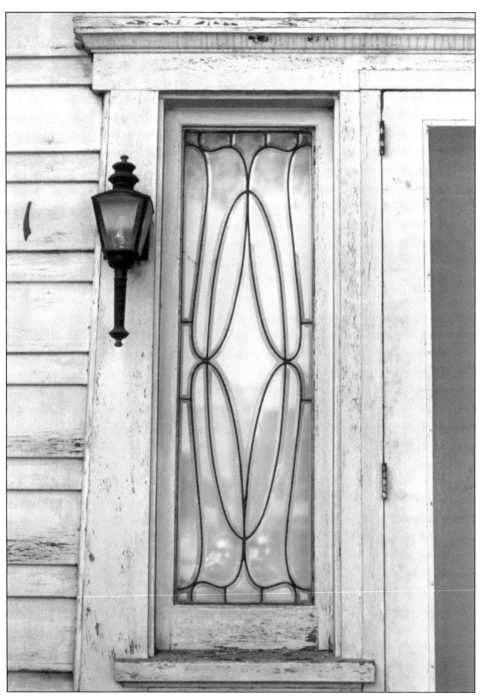

831 SOUTH IROLO STREET, MID-WILSHIRE. This leaded glass window flanking the front door has been replaced by a modern bay window. Undoubtedly, the builder or original owner selected it from a catalog of ready-made windows. These generally had an Art Nouveau or an Arts and Crafts feeling that seemed to suit the bungalow, but some were in frankly retrospective styles. Here, the window was perfectly intact, but the wear around it shows why someone thought to replace it. And yet, dirty as it was, it wore its age well.

551 North Hobart Boulevard, Hollywood. This striking chimney appears to be intact, perhaps because its unusual construction of concrete, rather than brick, enabled it to survive earthquakes. The textured surface, within a demure flat frame, is all the more striking when it flares out at the bottom. It is placed just where the main gable gives way to a flat roofline, between two windows. One wonders what problems its exaggerated form hides or whether it was just a fancy of the builder.

2155 West Twenty-Ninth Street, South Central. This simple house is intact on a street of intact bungalows, every one of which presents different interesting features. Two semicircular porch nooks are built of stone in two variations of basketwork patterns. They surround paired trapezoidal columns that support the front gable composed of a typical but very carefully balanced arrangement of main beam and purlins with beveled edges, serried up in symmetrical order to the art glass window. The house as a whole is one large tent gable. This neighborhood was a prime market for the Los Angeles Investment Company and other bungalow builders.

4545 MELBOURNE AVENUE, LOS FELIZ. Built in 1907, this house appears to be well-preserved. A long high gable pulls the eye up to windows snugly fit under the roofline amid a wall of diamond-shaped shingles. The small top window fronts a projecting attic. The shingle pattern, with horizontal courses separating the principal panels, is more "ornamental" than the simplicity that the bungalow usually insisted upon, but it still does not approach the clutter of Eastlake or Queen Anne–style facings. It is a house meant for a suburban neighborhood at the edge of the city, in what was a new development.

2443 FOURTH STREET, SANTA MONICA (ABOVE), AND 150 FRASER AVENUE, OCEAN PARK. These two intact houses are a few blocks apart. The structure on Fraser Avenue has been modernized and simplified; the fanciful coxcomb on top of the entry porch, which recalls the waves of the ocean that is just a block away from the house, is gone. The bungalows on this and adjacent blocks are long and deep rather than wide, due to the way that land is used near the ocean as opposed to inland tracts. And indeed, just a short way inland, the house on Fraser Avenue takes on the more generous horizontality of the classic bungalow, with tapering columns, a spreading eave, rafter ends, double gables, a long narrow ventilation aperture, and crosswise blocks atop the main beam.

336–342 ½ North Avenue 57, Highland Park. This bungalow court, built in 1921, remains a part of its neighborhood. Considerable effort was made in Los Angeles in the years following World War I to replace groups of shacks, built by owners rather than developers, that had appeared when the population of the region quadrupled in the first decades of the century. The bungalow style allowed inexpensive but high-quality small houses to be built in commercially viable ways, and the court was one such solution. Whereas these cottages are now behind a wall, their openness and simplicity, with many front-facing windows below jerkin-headed gables, were a part of the mood of Los Angeles at the time.

1701 ALTIVO WAY, ECHO PARK. Perched in a forgotten corner at the back of Echo Park, on a spur at the end of the long trail of Echo Park Avenue (near street number 2443), the photographer and his companion met the old lady who lived here in the small house her father built in 1913. Down the street had lived some of the most famous bohemian of Los Angeles during her youth—Jake Zeitlin (the photographer's great uncle), Lawrence Clark Powell, John Cage, and others. She had a huge view across the rail yards at the foot of the Echo Park Hills toward Eagle Rock. She invited the two curious strangers in, and there, they stepped into the Los Angeles of a half-century before.

1214 SOUTH ARAPAHOE STREET, SOUTH CENTRAL (ABOVE), AND 844–846 NORTH LAGUNA AVENUE, ECHO PARK. The house on Arapahoe Street has now been replaced by an apartment building, while the Echo Park house still proudly looks over the recently restored Echo Park Lake. The two houses are studies in duplex bungalows of impressive proportions with striking entrances. The house on Arapahoe Street was unique and not from a builder's plan. It is a duplex version of the "airplane" bungalow on stilts, as it were, with a "cockpit" for each side. The symmetry is nicely carried out by the paired columns and other details. The Echo Park bungalow remains a beautiful structure. Here, one large gable unites the two units and their symmetrical porches atop a sinuous brick staircase.

Two

BUNGALOWS IN DETAIL

Every one of the basic principles of modernist architecture is used in the bungalow. It is not in any retrospective style, assuming the decor of any age or nation the builder chooses. Rather, the bungalow is built in the style of the bungalow alone. Its decoration arises from the arrangement and exposure of some of its structural members. Braces and joints are commonly visible. These are treated as abstract lines in complex intersections. Porch supports, really bearing loads, are satisfying lines of beams, bricks, stones, or stucco. The bungalow has numerous extensions of the indoors to the outside along lines hugging the horizontal—wide porches sweeping from the front around the sides, eaves waving well below the line of the ceiling, gables exploding out on every side, and bows and bays puncturing the sides and rear. Almost every room has its own element or line shooting out from the house.

Up to its time, no mass-produced type of house rivaled the bungalow for its dynamic interiors. The front sitting room easily flows over and around a low partition to the dining room. Rooms are connected by bookcases lining the common wall or by a graceful wooden arch. The living room has its low rock fireplace, perhaps with an inglenook or pattern of tiles around it; the dining room has the drawers and shelves of its built-in sideboard. Indeed, bungalow designers invented the modern built-in to a large degree. Hallways often disappeared, leaving quick access to three or four bedrooms, perhaps grouped around a porch on the side or rear of the house, covered with a pergola handsomely composed of wooden posts and beams. A small second story, with windows all around, or an attic sometimes topped the house. The doors are generally striking simple slabs of wood with distinct rectangular lines emphasized by rectangular panels of beveled glass.

Beyond its visual interest, however, the bungalow had among its leading concepts, along with the influences of the Arts and Crafts movement and of the health fads of the day, a basic social principle in the founding of modern architecture. It was popular housing, capable of mass production, not designed for monumentality or eternity. Bungalows are never palaces. They were designed to treat each person in the masses as equal yet individual. On a street full of bungalows, the eye is constantly exercised by the welter of rooflines and by the motley of projecting and receding elements. Although many bungalows were based on a uniform plan, there are probably no two that are exactly alike.

566 SOUTH NORTON AVENUE, HANCOCK PARK. Like most of the others on this street of large bungalows, the house is well taken care of. Cheap bungalows cost less than $2,500 to build (some as little as $800), and these larger houses ran from $2,500 to $5,000. Generally, the posher structures had full second stories, whereas a single story is part of the concept of the canonical bungalow. The asymmetry of the upper story pulls the heart of the house to the side porch entrance, although a rough stone wall flanking the front door steps unites the facade horizontally. Curved profile rafter tails and open flat-cut fretwork under the long attic gable unite the house into a solid prosperous dwelling.

1377 MALTMAN AVENUE, SILVER LAKE. This is the second-story balcony door under a projecting eave. A later owner preserved the door railing and the shingled corners of the balcony but has rehabilitated the eave as well as repainted it, restoring the harmonious look of this capacious bungalow home. Silver Lake, south of Sunset Boulevard, was a patchwork development in which this 1911 house was one of the first to be built. With views of both downtown and the Pacific Ocean, it was a perfect fresh-air health-house, generously sized and detailed with projecting gables, half-timbering, and many windows, all promising the good life.

1377 MALTMAN AVENUE, SILVER LAKE. Recessed in an exterior shake wall, this perfectly symmetrical leaded glass panel has the touch of Arts and Crafts style that was used to add modest decorative touches to the sturdy masculine monochrome interiority of the bungalow.

1110 SOUTH ARAPAHOE STREET, MID-WILSHIRE (ABOVE), AND 4611 CLARISSA AVENUE, LOS FELIZ. Gables and porches were the hooks that made the bungalow seem large, comfortable, and modern. They suggested openness, and the way in which their structures were displayed was a core point at which design moved away from the plush-lined boxiness of the Victorian house. On South Arapahoe Street, built in 1912, a profusion of elongated gables, accentuated by open fretwork, sits high and to the back of a balcony on top of the long porch, supported by three brick piers that frame the verandah. In Los Feliz, the upper-story gable and window are perpendicular to those of the ground floor. A very large L-shaped porch is created by wooden supports for congruent eaves springing from a row of piers. Both houses use exaggerated scales, with one vertical and the other horizontal to draw the buyer into their dreams. Both houses are intact.

1752 Vista Del Mar Avenue, Hollywood. This is a telling detail. A square concrete corner pier sharply contrasts with the dark wood walls and roof and is flanked by two long widows with narrow rectangular cut-ups. Thus, in one spot, there are the solidity and low cost of concrete, the dominant wooden look, and the sense that nature and sunshine are brought into the home. Following the regrettable trend to turn the front yard of the house into a private room, thick, tall hedges, the current state of the property, though well cared for, has lost the simplicity and openness that were the style in what seemed to be the friendlier Los Angeles of 1914.

2125 West Twenty-Ninth Street, South Central. Elements remain, but the simple dentelle motif lining the bean of each porch gable has been lost, and the wood wall sidings of the house have been stuccoed. These gaping porch gables were a bit of an obsession for the house builder of this block. They are eloquent and yet weird but also perfectly ordinary narrow gables on fieldstone piers and supported by curving knee-brace brackets that accentuate their eccentric geometry. At right angles to one another, they make an interesting entrance and also hide the ventilation eave.

915 South Irolo Street, Mid-Wilshire. This house has been heavily modified. The front row of trapezoidal columns defining the front porch has been absorbed into the enclosures of each side of the porch into interior rooms, and the whole house is enclosed in stucco so that its character as a wooden structure has largely disappeared. The eyebrow gable remains, sheltering a balcony that is a vestige of the sleeping porches that were common in both bungalow and more modernist architecture of the time. As shown here, this 1911 house had charm, appearing larger than it is. But today, it has lost all of that.

4526 MELBOURNE AVENUE, LOS FELIZ. About a third of the left side of the porch has been removed, along with the large window to the left of the door. No resulting enlargement or improvement is visible. The house was, and still is, as seen here, an example of the eloquence of the simplest bungalow style: two strong, clean overlapping gables, with matching slatted attic ventilators, add up to a simple but effective sense of place in a one-story home.

1931 AND 1937 NORTH GRAMMERCY PLACE, HOLLYWOOD (ABOVE), AND 4973 PASADENA AVENUE TERRACE, HIGHLAND PARK. Both Hollywood houses, built in 1910, are beautifully maintained. Together, they show how strongly the rooflines of the bungalow could accentuate the site of the house, as here the street climbs to the Los Feliz foothills. Various elements in the bungalow kit—deep eaves, fanciful brackets, tapering columns—all work together. The generous windows and balconies, all still intact, take advantage of the upslope. The Highland Park house uses the same tools for a flat lot, where the simple congruent upswept gable peaks create a strong street identity.

214 NORTH BENTON WAY, CITY-CENTER. Part of a bungalow court, this intersection of porch rails in a clinker brick pier presents a close detail of the way materials were used to create space and handsome design. It recalls, on the one hand, simple log house construction and, on the other, the complex joinery that Greene and Greene, with their master carpenter Peter Hall, made into stunning architectural art for expensive houses.

708 Victoria Avenue, Venice. These symmetrical braces use function to decorate and warm the home. They surmount a typical array of variegated windows and a door. The thickness and evident bolting were necessary because they, along with thick brick columns, support a huge gable that dominates the street and shades a deep porch across the front and fully down the side of the house. This 1912 house is perfectly maintained.

250 SOUTH BENTON WAY, CITY-CENTER (ABOVE), AND 4526 MELBOURNE AVENUE, LOS FELIZ. Intersecting gables were often further varied by different shingle patterns, including over-sawed boards and half-shakes. On Benton Way, the eaves hide the attic ventilator opening, while on Melbourne Avenue they make it prominent. Although the bungalow is associated with warm, medium-value, and earth tones, photography in black and white shows how much the style played with line, volume, light, and shadow, created, as here, by large and small architectural elements.

2297 West Twenty-Fourth Street, South Central (Above), and 1023 West Kensington Road, Echo Park. Both houses are intact. On West Twenty-Fourth Street, the ventilators are screened by varying patterns of slats and capped by a joinery ornament. In the Echo Park house, the ventilators are hidden, and instead, the eye is completely drawn to the singular cut-ups of the pair of windows, scaled up and down not only under the eaves, but in the windows and the door all across the front of the home. The motif is actually Victorian, recalling open screening of rooms by vertical railings; but here, it becomes an expressive simple functional element.

1306–1310 SUNSET BOULEVARD, ELYSIAN HEIGHTS. This remarkable survivor of the bungalow court fad attests to the keen commercial instinct behind it. These tiny and nearly crude apartments, built for transients, now cost a lot of money to rent as they trade on the bohemian history of the neighborhood. On one side, huge apartment blocks loom over it; the other side has a still-vacant lot and a row of old one-story commercial buildings that maintain the character of the street.

1985 NORTH VAN NESS AVENUE, HOLLYWOOD (ABOVE), AND 825 SOUTH KINGSLEY AVENUE, MID-WILSHIRE. The series of recessed volumes in these two houses show both the way that the bungalow style could be adapted to lot shape, as in the house on Van Ness Avenue, and the way it could add character to a standard lot. The house on South Kingsley Avenue has been demolished and replaced with an ugly apartment building.

546 SOUTH NORTON, HANCOCK PARK. These two leaded glass windows at right angles on the corner of the structure reflect one another and are transparent to one another. This, in turn, reflects the intersecting roof and beamlines of the front porch—a pleasantly witty articulation of the relationship between interior and exterior.

2302 WEST TWENTY-FIFTH STREET, SOUTH CENTRAL. This window, faintly echoing a bit of Gothic Revival, is a large and prominent element in a large and striking two-story bungalow home. The house commands a big corner lot with a wraparound porch in front and a wide porte cochère in back. The two-story-high window is part of a large room projected out under a gable supported by fanciful brackets that, in turn, are congruent with a much wider gable, with the same brackets and a smaller version of this window off to the side; other large gables and square windows complete the exterior, which, nonetheless, centers on this impressive set-piece side window.

4525 AND 4531 MELBOURNE AVENUE, LOS FELIZ. The steep upper-story gable, giving on to a prominent dormer, visually interlocks with the rooflines of the neighboring house. This is a strong illustration of the architectural coherence that a group of adjacent bungalows produced. The awning and landscaping enrich the neighborliness of these houses, built in 1910, rather than isolate them. The photograph also shows the strength of contrasting lines that make bungalow architecture photogenic.

2812 Oregon Street, Boyle Heights. The three front gables pictured here, echoed by an angled bracing over the front porch, have now lost their detail; the house is stucco, and the porch has been enclosed.

1719 Pleasant Avenue, Boyle Heights. The deep front and balcony porches, framed by two courses of paired square columns and a repeated pattern of doubled rafters, are gone; a brick apartment block has replaced this bungalow duplex, with its perfect bilateral symmetry.

1116 SOUTH ELDEN AVENUE, SOUTH CENTRAL. Built in 1913, the ground-floor rooms on either side of the front door were probably open porches when constructed. A pattern of paired double supports is carried through on the balcony along the whole front. The roofline, however, varies, with a gable on one half and a low-hipped dormer on the other creating a visually pleasing apartment house.

1359 NORTH LA BREA AVENUE, HOLLYWOOD. The strength of standard bungalow decorative joinery is readily seen here. A stone-faced pier supports a decorated wooden capitol, topped by two sets of double blocks under double main beams for the front porch with intersecting rafters. A gable sets off the whole structure, which includes three other very similar porch supports.

1359 North La Area Avenue, Hollywood. This house, built in 1911, is now in a state of advanced dilapidation. The property is fenced off, and considering the wave of capital development on this part of La Area Avenue, an extremely valuable location such as this will very likely be filled by a large retail and residential building. In 1976, its decline was already evident. Massage parlors were a kind of brothel commonly seen on older city streets in the late 1970s.

1636–1639 ½ North Morton Avenue, Echo Park. Two porches, up and down stairs, bring shade and depth to a very simple but very welcoming house. The whitewashed wooden balustrades of this 1911 bungalow seem to pull in all the bright summer light from around the house to rest peaceably with a calm, sheltered life within the home.

1636–1639 NORTH MORTON AVENUE, ECHO PARK. This simple window fully expresses the relation of the bungalow to its world. It is simple but decorative, frankly public but cozy and inward. It is a work of direct and pure art and also utterly functional. The two tapering sides of the frame support a small model of the most common bungalow woodworking motif. Built in 1911, it has been demolished and replaced.

1117 NORTH DOUGLAS STREET, ECHO PARK. This early shingled bungalow, built in 1909 in the Swiss style, was probably designed by the owner-builder, as nothing similar is to be found in books of plans for sale. It commands a split-level site on an upsloping street in a neighborhood thickly built up in the decades before 1940.

1117 North Douglas Street, Echo Park. A long balcony between square brick pillars subtends the upper story capped by a wide and deep gable at the top over a symmetrical row of windows; the gable is perched on sets of five beams of decreasing length. This is a large home, now shabby but intact, made larger by converting the lower level into a room fronted by a porch.

401 Ocean Avenue, Santa Monica. This beautiful bungalow once occupied one of the choicest lots in all of California; right across from the Palisades at the shore of the Pacific, a few blocks from downtown Santa Monica. A five-sided bay window looked at the water.

DETAIL OF 401 OCEAN AVENUE, SANTA MONICA. Behind the bay window another wing was formed by gables at an oblique angle, and a projecting second story on double rafters was centered on the chimney. While large apartment buildings have filled most of the nearby oceanfront lots, this has been replaced by a large house constructed as five condominiums.

719 Forest Avenue, Boyle Heights (Above), and 5428 Aldama Street, Highland Park. The shake, shingle, and over-sawn sidings of early bungalows are both the largest part of the structure as its "skin" and the most vulnerable to damage and, therefore, to replacement. Wood siding requires regular maintenance and replacement. The most common and saddest adulteration of the bungalow that one regularly sees is the wood exterior being replaced by stucco in the postwar period. Cedar, pine, spruce, and redwood are the most common woods for shakes, which are split off from the log; shingles, which are sawn smooth; and for sawn board siding much like clapboard though applied by a different technique.

365 NORTH WILTON PLACE, HOLLYWOOD (ABOVE, LEFT); 2434 FOURTH STREET, SANTA MONICA (ABOVE, RIGHT); AND 633 CAMULOS STREET, BOYLE HEIGHTS (BELOW). The examples here were chosen for the variety and expressiveness of their patterns. The two houses on the preceding page are opposites; one is completely irregular and entertaining, while the other is deep and rigidly regular. On this page, one sees regular patterns built up of courses of alternating length, length narrowing up the wall, and a mix of motley and repetition.

402 Avenue 57, Highland Park. The Highland Park neighborhood was built up early, as development extended first northeast and southwest from downtown rather than west. This house was a top-of-the-line two-story bungalow, with a sleeping porch and dining bay. The stepped profile of the chimney echoes the structure of the front stairs stonework, itself extended into the two high stone piers supporting the large front beam and framing a basket-pattern stone porch rail (not visible). The emphatic front access and the single-beam porch, along with the carefully detailed roof gable features, were elements that constructed the appeal of costlier bungalows.

DETAIL OF 401 AVENUE 57, HIGHLAND PARK. This detail of support for the long porch beam shows a vernacular adaptation of the knee brace to support a very heavy beam by reinforcing it. The reinforcement element is artless—just a thick stick of wood—but it matches the reserved curve of the brace. Both are chunky and uncomplicated. They add to the homespun image of the bungalow, created to appeal to a do-it-yourself aesthetic.

551 South Kingsley Drive, Mid-Wilshire. The viewer will readily infer from this elaborate doorway that it is part of a large and opulent house. Built in 1911, this three-story bungalow is the longtime home of the Southern California chapter of the Women's Christian Temperance Union. The paneling of the door uses the smooth stepped arrangement of horizontal wooden elements that are nearly universal in local bungalows, despite Queen Anne detailing of the house as a whole. The door centers a long brick-fronted porch under a typical bungalow braced gable.

226 Palisades Avenue, Santa Monica. Henry Greene, who, with his brother Charles as Greene and Greene designed some of the greatest and most famous houses of the early 20th century, was the architect of this huge 1917 house. It sits intact in a street of well-kept homes that are part of the Santa Monica bungalow town. All the elements of the door decor, frame, gable, and setting are more vertical than bungalow design usually is.

6054 SELMA AVENUE, HOLLYWOOD. This stretch of Selma Avenue is a generally intact Hollywood "bungalowtown," while other parts of the street have completely changed. This porch beam support is elegant and functional. Mortise and tenon subtend the beam, which, in turn, braces the gable. The logic of it crosses amateur and professional carpentry. And its attractiveness, even when unpainted, exemplifies what Mike Davis calls the miniaturization of the Arroyo aesthetic, referring to the Arroyo Seco in Pasadena that many of the great Greene and Greene houses and other adaptations around the bungalow style took over.

5100 Harold Way, Hollywood. Still in what remains of the Hollywood bungalowtown, this 1909 house shows a curious specimen of the style. A group of blocks imitates the mortice and tenon joinery on the facia of the pillar. They, in turn, are part of another false display, the mirrored carved blocks that seem to support a porch beam although they are not in visible contact with it. In fact, the pillar alone carries the whole load. The result is visually rather satisfying, even provocative, with a certain chattering busy eloquence, seen also in the weird rafter tail. But the working parts are more ordinary, so that, again, the aesthetic refers the homeowner and viewer to the larger field of design without incurring its expense.

**886 North Lafayette Park Place,
Silver Lake.** All these details frame
a very deep front porch, emphasizing
the porch as the signifier of the cozy
but "affordable" 1911 bungalow home.
These rafters are cheaply finished, being
simply sawed off in both the single
and double-layer fringes in front and
on the side. The main beam is not as
large as it might be and is supported
on a pair of double columns. The very
slightly upswept ends of the gable give
a distant whiff of the pagoda motif.

972 NORTH NORMANDIE AVENUE, HOLLYWOOD. The property was demolished and replaced by a group of apartment blocks. The porch was flanked by thick stucco pillars with decorative brick panels. Ascending slightly pyramidal wooden elements finish the main beam support, with a fringe of beveled rafter tails above.

DETAIL OF 972 NORTH NORMANDIE AVENUE, HOLLYWOOD. All of this creates porch shadows on the alternating long and short shingles. A rail guards the porch, and the chimney carries the motif up above the roof. The sense of a solid home, crafted to be distinctive, was, however superficial, more human than the housing that eliminated it.

1221–1223 EAST FORTIETH PLACE, WATTS. This house, a Los Angeles Historic-Cultural Monument since 1976 and listed in the National Register of Historic Places since 1978, was the home of Dr. Ralph Bunche, the first person of color to win a Nobel Peace Prize. By 1990, it was so derelict that it came close to being torn down. Built in 1931, now restored and in private hands, it is a "tent bungalow" under one peaked roof structure, with an ample porch. The dog came to his perch in the window to inspect the photographer just when he was ready to leave.

102 SOUTH KINGSLEY DRIVE, MID-WILSHIRE. Simple elements create an effective image in bungalows that presents both domesticity and a sense of intentional beauty. The window, a bungalow standard like others shown here, gracefully fits the wall of shake it sits in, while the shadow line of the gable situates the assemblage. The image itself uses the grayscale of black-and-white photography to convey the earth tones of the bungalow materials. Built in 1915, the house has a chimney and three large, square, field stone pillars.

953 SOUTH IROLO STREET, MID-WILSHIRE. This house has been demolished; the lot is now a playground. This front porch gable, with a pronounced pagoda peak, is supported by a symmetrical arrangement of beams joined at right angles in a way that attracts somewhat startled interest because it looks rickety and readily collapsible. It is in fact intended to be part of the "Japanese" effect signified by the gable motif.

211 East Twenty-Ninth Street, South Central. This home has been demolished and replaced by an apartment building. Shot from an angle that emphasizes its oddity, the house wall here has a narrow bay of unusual shape next to a small gable mysteriously nestled under the main gable. All parts of the structure are supported on rafters with the same style of double tail.

741 South Irolo Street, Mid-Wilshire (Above, Left); 972 South Wilton Place, Mid-Wilshire (Above, Right); 939 South Ardmore Avenue, Mid-Wilshire (Below, Left); and 531 North Hobart Boulevard, Hollywood (Below, Right). All four of these doors have disappeared, and only one of the houses is extant. The house on Irolo Street was designed by Arthur and Alfred Heineman (see page 23). Doors generally were ordered from catalogs, with the result that (as with decorative glass windows and interior tile panels) they sometimes had decor that was out of sympathy with bungalow style, as on Wilton Place. But in each of these cases, the settings of the doors incorporate them into the aesthetic—recessed in a porch, against a shingled wall, under a gable with clearly articulated structural elements. The adjacent window on Ardmore Avenue and the panels on either side of the doors Irolo Street and Wilton Place emphasize the ground-hugging horizontality of the street faces.

1359 NORTH MALTMAN, SILVER LAKE (ABOVE, LEFT); 4757 OAKWOOD AVENUE, HOLLYWOOD (ABOVE, RIGHT); 245 NORTH WILTON PLACE, HOLLYWOOD (BELOW, LEFT); AND 2443 ECHO PARK AVENUE, ECHO PARK (BELOW, RIGHT). All but the last of these doors have disappeared, and the first two houses have been demolished. As above, Oakwood Avenue uses a cut glass design from a fussier aesthetic, and the last door has the most purely Arts and Crafts inspiration. Raymond Chandler said that anyone could easily break into houses in Los Angeles through any part of them except the front door, solid and impregnable but surrounded by windows and patio entrances that could easily be jimmied open.

2258 West Twenty-Fourth Street, South Central. In the middle of the huge bungalowtown that extends south and southwest of downtown, now called South Central, this symmetrical two-story bungalow uses double columns, double supports, double gables, double windows, and a central balcony. Uncomplicated detailing and a prominent rafter fringe made this large single-family home attractive to its original purchaser in 1909 who saw it as distinctive but staid, arising along straight streets made from old bean fields into a middle-class neighborhood.

4655 Maplewood Avenue, Hollywood. This is a really beautiful specimen of a large bungalow in a pure style, now, sadly, replaced by an apartment block. Both stories present full-width balconies, organized by the same structure of double uprights carried up both floors. The gable work is similar to the "airplane" style, with a low central setback "cockpit." Built as a duplex, the house is set back in just the right perspective.

1346 North Fairfax Avenue, West Hollywood. Surviving against the odds since 1919, the house is now drowned by the steady development of upper Fairfax Avenue. This type of bungalow was often called "colonial" (note the fan window above the door), a style that might have been more comfortable and familiar to the retirees from the Midwest who came to Southern California to "live in little bungalows, with a palm-tree or banana plant in front, and eat in cafeterias," as Louis Adamic put it.

2032 Sixth Street, Santa Monica (Above), and 2102 Sixth Street, Santa Monica. The timid bay on Sixth Street was much less common than the more assertive bay that appears in many bungalows. These two bays on different houses a block from each other are almost identical. But, as so often in bungalows, the details individuate them. The windows differ in number and style, and the shingle fringes below also differ, but in both, a fringe of rafter tails sets off the room.

844 Laguna Avenue, Echo Park. This one detail has square brick piers, a curved knee brace, complex joinery gable supports in typical style, the main porch beam, vertical ventilation louvers, eaves on rafters, and gables just visible on the side. Additionally, the whole house is a symmetrical duplex, now well-maintained, with two gabled structures of this sort and porches, set atop a curving brick staircase from the street level. Black-and-white photography picks up the way the shadows of the porch intersect the light reflected off the whitewashed carpentry.

4631 Welch Place, Los Feliz. Here, the knee brace is anchored to the side of the brick pier rather than springing off from on top of it. Rafters with flared ends are built up by mortice and tenon to support the porch beam. Although there are quite a few well-tended bungalows on this small street, this house no longer exists.

1224 NORTH POINSETTIA PLACE, HOLLYWOOD (ABOVE), AND 1251 NORTH MARIPOSA AVENUE, HOLLYWOOD. While Poinsettia Place (built in 1921) is a "colonial" bungalow and Mariposa Avenue (built in 1919) is a more standard bungalow, they share the same basic elements. They are boxy, street-facing, one-story structures, without the contrasting planes of more expensive bungalows. In both, the rafters of a shallow front porch are extended to create pergolas on either side of the centered door. By contrast, the gable of the colonial uses pointed rafter tails and fanciful brackets in the standard style, whereas the other, while using nested gables for a bungalow effect, converts the porch gable into an open pediment.

1636 NORTH STANLEY AVENUE, WEST HOLLYWOOD. Built in 1920, this house certainly came straight out of a plan book. In the photograph, it looks almost as bare as it was when its first occupants moved in, although now it is a bit rundown and overgrown by shrubbery in a neighborhood of very expensive well-restored bungalows and older homes of similar date. The front is a flat line of three French doors behind a pergola on round columns, echoed by a long, narrow attic dormer.

325 SAN VICENTE BOULEVARD, SANTA MONICA. This house has been demolished. Brickwork in bungalows is often unappreciated because of the prominence of carpentry. Here, some clinker brick is used along with a dominant pattern of bricks in varying shades to create dynamic small stairs with balustrade curving up from square piers.

327 NORTH OXFORD STREET, HOLLYWOOD. This appealing house has been demolished. Wood blocks in a crisscross pattern lead up to both a beam enclosing a glazed porch and a brace supporting the main gable, with a pointed rafter tail that somehow pulls together the whole composition. With the small tree and potted plants, it has the well-lived look that bungalows strove to achieve.

20 Park Avenue, Venice. This house is in immaculate condition, as well it might be given the prices in Venice today. Yet in 1911, when this house was built, few would have thought that any part of Venice would be a neighborhood of multimillion dollar houses. Shortly after Abbot Kinney built Venice in 1905 as a simulacrum of Old World culture, initiated with grotesquely massive publicity, he converted it to a seashore honky-tonk circus because no one came for the culture. Most canals were filled in, and bungalows began to appear where palazzi were supposed to stand. The development of the bungalow style here was solid proof that the Victorianism of Los Angeles architecture before 1900 was deceased. With its high gable and curving balcony under a wooden awning in style at a contrasting angle, on a fine walk street, this bungalow continues to be a fresh and pleasant home, much extended in the back.

220 SOUTH WILTON PLACE, MID-WILSHIRE. Rooflines of two stories on three planes plus one side of a six-sided conical tower and a side gable intersect here around exposed rafter ends, applied decor, and decorative windows. The cacophony is engaging, and yet when one looks at the whole house, all these elements harmonize, being set back from the street to the advantage of the whole composition.

1901 NORTH RODNEY DRIVE, HOLLYWOOD. This bungalow is now demolished, like every other original house on this side of the whole length of the street, in favor of 1980s apartment complexes. These congruent jerkin-headed gables, with a dormer at a right angle to them, shade ample windows covering almost the whole ground floor. The decorative brackets of the upper story and the exposed rafters on both floors emphasize the earth-hugging lines of the bungalow home.

501 NORTH HOBART BOULEVARD, HOLLYWOOD. Flat cut-out forms were common ways to vary balcony railings as well as ventilators. This house has been demolished.

1904 NORTH BERKELEY AVENUE, ECHO PARK. The attic ventilation apertures that the one-story bungalow required helped to cool the house before air-conditioning since the heat of Southern California made the climate less salubrious than it was advertised to be. Here, a sunrise pattern compliments the tinker-toy framing of the porch, which today looks as fresh as the day it was built in 1920.

929 NORTH NORMANDIE AVENUE, HOLLYWOOD (ABOVE), AND 2215 WEST 24TH STREET, SOUTH CENTRAL. These two houses share similar strong gables defining their volumes, symmetrically around a central front door in one case and asymmetrically with the front door to the side in the other. In both, the second-story overhang shades the porch. The first house was never restored from the condition in which it was photographed in 1976 and has been replaced by a bunker of unspeakable ugliness.

433 CASANOVA STREET, CHINATOWN. This house has been demolished and replaced by apartments. Essentially a hill cabin, it was built on the side of Elysian Heights, which was, at the time, suburban, adjacent to the historic core. In fact, few bungalows were constructed this close to downtown, where Victorian houses and commercial buildings dominated. Its chief architectural interest is the zigzag gable line, pulled outward to shade a veranda, and then topped by a yet deeper sidewise gable behind the porch, all framing a nice row of windows. As crude as it is, it has a sense of place.

886 North Lafayette Park Place, Silver Lake. The attention paid to pergolas in bungalow houses reflected the obsession with the abundance of the supposed "subtropical" climate of Southern California. "Subtropical" was the real estate salesman's invention and come-on. On hillsides such as that which Lafayette Park Place climbs, the thick old groves of live oak were quickly chopped down in order to provide views, which in time the new eucalyptus and pines obscured. Next, native manzanita, ribes, buckthorn, and ceanothus were replaced by bougainvillea, jasmine, and other imported shrubs and bedding plants that conveyed an image of lush verdure and, beneath it, the message that California had healing powers expressed in its fertility.

2096 West Twenty-Ninth Street, South Central. This detail seems to have been lost from the only "updated" house on a block of otherwise well-preserved and interesting bungalows. These pointed rafter tails, crossed where two sides of the house meet at a stone porch pier, show off the visual interest that lines and shadows create in unassuming bungalows.

Three

THINKING IN BUNGALOW

The authors of the bungalow style are mostly unknown; their work was anonymous, behind the plans for sale published by builders, some of whom might have been designers but who by and large employed draftsmen to do the work. Of all the houses in this book, the names of the architects of just two of them are known: the famous brothers Greene designed the house on page 68, and the brothers Heineman designed the house on page 23. In some known cases, the builder was a carpenter or a shipwright who simply constructed a house for his family. But it was mostly the employees of the developers who made the plans for tract after tract of bungalows, designed with an eye to flexibility and modest construction costs. The plans could be "individualized" for each buyer. The innate popularity of the style, expressed in the democratic anonymity of its design, bestowed on professionals and amateurs alike, provided a measure of freedom and unconventionality. These qualities were restricted by the ideology of middle-class coziness, but even the great architects of the day, such as Irving Gill, also struggled against bourgeois conventionality.

Between 1900 and about 1930, some of the best architectural ideas of New York, Chicago, Vienna, and Berlin were instantiated on a popular scale in Los Angeles. They were interpreted by the developers who added their cosmopolitism to the more homely virtues they boasted of in their products. Thus, the modernist design principles became part of the flimflam of the boisterous growth of Los Angeles. To these houses came young families and old retirees from LaGrange and Cleveland, seeking health, space, decency, and jobs. They included as well the stagestruck from all over America, seeking fame, beauty, and riches. As the labors of all these sustained and encouraged the exploding city, its tracts of open land were gradually replaced by tracts of bungalows, full of children, grandchildren, furniture, and pets. The bungalows were the naive, commodious, and successful boomtown houses of this commodified, broad, flat, hot, and open city.

4973 SYCAMORE AVENUE TERRACE, HIGHLAND PARK. Window boxes, like sleeping porches, were another device for "bringing the outdoors indoors"—a feature that even the snobbiest critics of the bungalow liked. It was related to various health movements that thrived in Southern California and still do. Greene and Greene houses extensively developed the concept, which, in turn, became a commonplace of Mid-century Modernism after the Schindler-Neutra house of 1922 in West Hollywood centered them. The composition of this house is precise; the window cut-ups echo the shingle shapes, and the box supports carry up the porch covering from below.

571 Cypress Avenue, Highland Park. The striking design of this 1911 house has been tastefully maintained. In this photograph, the eye is drawn to the unusual wraparound second-story sleeping porch and the many windows in frames of a typical design that open onto it. The shingles mimic the stone piers that, with a basketwork partial wall, define a ground-floor porch that is even longer than the upper story porch, also wrapping around the side. Many exposed beam ends and elaborate stairs and retaining walls of arroyo stone give the house some grandeur.

2434 FOURTH STREET, SANTA MONICA. This large 1915 bungalow duplex has a static, completely symmetrical street elevation, in which simple details are carried throughout the woodwork.

2143 NORTH CANYON DRIVE, HOLLYWOOD. This is a beautiful 1910 house, built in the first years of the "Hollywoodland" tracts. A column-supported gable porch entrance is visually separated from the main gable, below which the long, gently curving bay window sits. This leads to the elements at the side of the house. The attic ventilators of each eave use a different cut-out slat pattern. This style of composition on a large lot suggests a compound or casually linked pavilions.

563–565 North Kenmore Avenue, Hollywood. This chimney hugged the ground, despite being a vertical element, by means of the Prairie-style brick detailing of its three-stepped profile. Furthermore, it was part of the front porch, with the bricks integrated with the shingles to create a sweet sense of place. This property has been demolished.

2424 FOURTH STREET, SANTA MONICA. This four-columned support and its mate support a wide low gable, backed up by two other gables at the same angles, in an airplane configuration. The four horizontal blocks with beveled ends intersect the uprights at a height in the right proportion for the building, held in by tenons, and are placed on a carefully assembled platform on top of the porch rail.

209 NORTH VENICE BOULEVARD, VENICE. This apartment house survives, as improbable as that might seem from this 1976 photograph, in which it looks near tilting over. The window boxes have been removed, as has the side door on the left and the fire escapes. Behind it is a three-story row of rental units, accessed by a long, narrow staircase and built in exactly the same style, although their actual date is undetermined. As it was in 1976, the many decorative rafters and fascia made this building both compelling and charming. The dusty Volvo in front and the then vacant lots on either side, both now built up, portray the bohemian Venice of its day.

978 SOUTH WILTON PLACE, MID-WILSHIRE (ABOVE), AND 986 SOUTH ARAPAHOE STREET, MID-WILSHIRE. Both of these impressive two-story bungalow homes have been demolished. On South Arapahoe Street, torn down within the last few years, the stone porch pillars rise all the way up and have no woodwork. Its low dormers and high-peaked gables create a strong image. In the Wilton Place house, the angled stairs, the deep top-story eaves, the second-story overhang, the rafter end fringe, and the window boxes turn a basic design into an interesting and pleasing street definer.

6145 CARLOS AVENUE, HOLLYWOOD. Posts and beams of equal and unequal dimensions join the pergola, porch, and gables. They create appealing shadows as well as the visual intrigue of a Jenga puzzle. Exposing structure as ornament was cheap and effective.

915 SOUTH IROLO STREET, MID-WILSHIRE. The house remains, though in rough shape and stuccoed over, but this marvelous part of it has disappeared. When it was built in 1911, however, it must have been a selling point. It signified the healthy outdoors life in which the buyer participated and expressed the values of the Arts and Crafts, Shingle style, and bungalow movements. Double posts and rounded-off crossbeams were all that was necessary to create an outdoor room.

2504 THIRD STREET, SANTA MONICA (ABOVE), AND 129 SOUTH KINGSLEY DRIVE, MID-WILSHIRE.
Built in 1909 and 1910, these houses show two treatments of dormers as "cozy" elements within
the bungalow vocabulary. Curved rooflines along the main gables in both houses enclose modest
traditional dormers in one house and an aggressively wide dormer in the other. Note the mix of
trapezoidal wooden columns and brick piers with other decor and the curved second-story rafter
tails echoing the roofline of the Kingsley house. Both houses use their main and side gables
effectively to create a strong street-side impression of the domestic spaces within.

6067 HAROLD WAY, HOLLYWOOD (ABOVE), AND 1200 SOUTH MAGNOLIA AVENUE, MID-WILSHIRE.
Rafters, posts, beams, braces, and purlins unify the housefront on Harold Way, built in 1938 and
now converted into a triplex, but fragment it on South Magnolia Avenue, now demolished. In
one case, they focus on the porch for a modest home, while in the other they make a larger home
appear rambling and spacious.

1034 West Kensington Road, Echo Park. Long beams create a very deep front porch, shading the door while diverting access to the side of the porch rather than straight up from the street. A large room fills the overhang. This 1903 house—built in one of the earliest important suburban tracts, Angelino Heights, developed by Prudent Beaudry—remains intact.

1377 North Maltman Avenue, Silver Lake. This is a detail from the house pictured here as No. 22. As in No. 98, a deep porch brings the outside and the inside close together, extending as a porte cochère on the left and repeated as a balcony from the room, filling the overhang above the porch. Repeated patterns of beams in a row, imaginatively finished, with strong double posts on brick piers and other decorative elements, root the bungalow to the lot from which occupants have views of downtown from the front and all the way to the ocean from the back.

905 SOUTH IROLO STREET, MID-WILSHIRE. Engulfed by apartment buildings on both sides, this 1908 house is representative of the kind of simple and cheap bungalow that filled up the neighborhood in the first two decades of the last century. But in 1928, decades after it was erected, a large brick apartment building in the pseudo-Spanish style went up next to it on vacant land. In 1990, another apartment building in the late dingbat style on the other side claimed an old bungalow. The bungalow man's sales pitch of a bungalowtown was hardly ever realized, as higher land values and changing tastes quickly overcame the appeal of the bungalow.

1917 North Grammercy Place, Hollywood. In contrast to the image on page 112, this 1912 bungalow has now been enhanced by a fieldstone wall and other improvements. But in 1976, it was not yet a multimillion dollar property. It was still a house for working-class people and families. A wide front verandah under a proscenium arch and an equally wide upstairs dormer with a balcony was, with the interior features and a television antenna, just enough for the times.

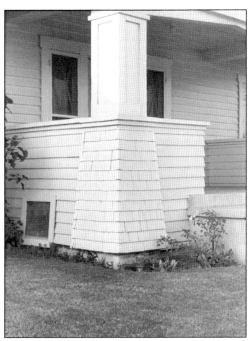

215 SOUTH BENTON WAY, CITY CENTER (ABOVE, LEFT); 1701 ALTIVO WAY, ECHO PARK (ABOVE, RIGHT); 551 SOUTH KINGSLEY DRIVE, MID-WILSHIRE (BELOW, LEFT); AND 219 NORTH WILTON PLACE, HOLLYWOOD (BELOW, RIGHT). Here are four treatments of corner piers, three of which are trapezoidal. The pier on Altivo Way is engaged. The group also shows an array of claddings or finishes—shingles, boards, wood and stucco, and brick—as well as a sampler from the decorative options for the bungalow, all of which are intended to express the structure in a pleasing way suited to the overall style.

434 North Kenmore Avenue, Hollywood. Although the house itself has been drowned in stucco, its front yard paved as a car park, and all the wood trim painted in the same brown as the house, this detail remains. As seen here, it is stunning—a contrast perfect in its simplicity, catching the light. The element links the porch to the gable but really does little to support the roof. Instead, it chiefly displays two beams with ends curved in opposite directions across double posts as an emblem of bungalow style through a core motif.

1100 Coronado Terrace, Echo Park. The collection of planes in the design takes full advantage of the views from the slope on which it is sited and gives a sense of amplitude to the building. A bay under a fringed of rafter tails extends to the left, while another wing emerges from behind on the right. Between these, the main gable shades an ample porch, and a second "captain's cabin" gable ties the elements together from the upper story. The porch base, piers, and railing are stone atop a stacked stone staircase.

2302 West Twenty-Fifth Street, South Central. Here is the whole house, one part of which is seen on page 50. Built in 1905 and sitting on a half-acre corner lot, the house is on a diagonal, with its front gate and door facing the intersection, the house mixes the upstanding bourgeois suburban villa with the bungalow.

2301 West Twenty-Fourth Street, South Central. The builder here exaggerated the pagoda peak motif in the gables, set against a similarly hyperbolic roofline. The bungalow style could accommodate eccentricity, but houses like this fought the conformist domesticity of the style.

1153–1155 ½ East Fortieth Place, Watts. This modest duplex was built in the waning days of the bungalow fad, in 1926. Nonetheless, two linked small gables sitting as branches of a one-story main gable, although plain when seen from straight on in front, form a visually active and interesting arrangement that makes the small porches appealing.

102 SOUTH KINGSLEY DRIVE, MID-WILSHIRE. Three large trapezoidal piers, a wall, and a massive chimney all of arroyo rocks define the volume of the structure on its corner lot. The piers support an arrangement of finished wood elements in the purest bungalow style. Although deep in the middle of the city even when it was built in 1915, the stonework and open gable structure signify the cultural basics of the bungalow—an affinity with nature, an informal meeting with the street, and well-cushioned working-class domesticity.

2420 NORTH GOWER, HOLLYWOOD. Although the 1918 house remains and has been enlarged, this lovely structure appears to have been lost. Pairs of sloping uprights create a gateway, mimicking a Japanese temple, perched over a driveway sloping down the side of the hill in the oldest part of the Hollywood Hills to which the house clings.

978 North Everett Street, Elysian Heights (Above), and 708 Victoria Avenue, Venice.
Bungalow style uses simple variations on the arrangements of gabled volumes to create varied spaces that have varying cultural and social signifiers. On Everett Street, the main gable oversees two congruent parallel gables atop a split-level porch formed by coursed stone-clad piers. On Victoria Avenue, the second-story gable is transverse to the wide front gable and its open and welcoming porch. This represents neighborly domesticity, whereas the house above stands up and away from the street but, nonetheless, does not pull away from being part of its neighborhood. Built in 1922 (above) and 1912 (below), these houses have been well maintained.

2813 OREGON STREET, BOYLE HEIGHTS (ABOVE), AND 1223–1225 EAST FIFTY-NINTH STREET, WATTS. These two simple houses remain but have not been well treated; the house on Oregon Street has been stuccoed. It was built by the father of the owner 56 years before this photograph was made. He was a friendly man who chatted with two curious strangers for a while from his plain front porch.

2466 ECHO PARK AVENUE, ECHO PARK. Nestled way at the end of Echo Park Avenue, in a corner of the city that seems not to have been touched by time, the rooms of this house are splayed at oblique angles. Each is under its own low-hipped roof as if it were a cabin or observatory in the mountains. The wide window frames intensify the sense of interiority. This is the bungalow at its most appealing—protective, wide-eyed, simple, and democratic.

1602–1610 Altivo Way, Echo Park. These "bungalowettes," built in 1920 in the same neighborhood as the house on page 124 and several other houses here, are adapted to their hillside street by a clever plan. Each segment is under one gable, and the gables are nested in a precise straight line up the slope. A large, open porch fronts the structure. Large, interesting windows in style and parallel rafter fringes complete the decoration.

THE LOS ANGELES INVESTMENT COMPANY. The Los Angeles Investment Company, the largest bungalow builders of its day, used this advertisement in its *Practical Bungalows: Typical California Homes, with plans* (1912), which presented its plans for bungalows costing more the $2,500, as well as in its *Inexpensive Bungalows*, of the same year, for bungalows costing less than $2,500. The company's "Gold Notes" were its top-of-liner come-on. This and its other techniques and forms of deposit aimed to make it easy for a wage earner to save the funds needed to build a bungalow home. By investing in the home building of others, the company maintained that anyone could build capital sufficient for buying a house. Indeed, the company did finance the construction of many working-class or junior executive bungalows, and it employed numerous people in the building trades in its own mills. But the gold in the Gold Notes glittered falsely. As a banking institution, the company was little more than a pyramid scheme. Its collapse threatened another real estate crash like the disaster of 1889.

BIBLIOGRAPHY

Adamic, Louis. *Laughing in the Jungle*. New York: Harper and Brothers, 1932.

Banham, Reyner. Los Angeles: *The Architecture of Four Ecologies*. Berkeley: University of California Press, 2001.

Brownstein, Ronald. *Rock Me on the Water: The Year Los Angeles Transformed Movies, Music, Television, and Politics*. New York: Harper, 2021.

Cobos, Karen Marie. *California Bungalow: A Landscape of Changing Values*. Master's Thesis. California State University at Fullerton, 1997.

Davis, Mike. *City of Quartz*. New York: Vintage, 1992.

Duchsherer, Paul. *The Bungalow: America's Arts and Crafts Home*. New York: Penguin Studio, 1995.

Gish, Todd. "Bungalow Court Housing in Los Angeles, 1900–1930: Top-down Innovation? Or Bottom-up Reform?" *Southern California Quarterly*, Vol. 91, No. 4 (2009–2010): 365–387.

Hernandez, Kim. "The 'Bungalow Boom': The Working-Class Housing Industry and the Development and Promotion of Early Twentieth-Century Los Angeles." *Southern California Quarterly*, Vol. 92, No. 4 (2010–2011): 351–392.

Hines, Thomas S. *Architecture of the Sun: Los Angeles Modernism, 1900–1970*. New York: Rizzoli, 2010.

Los Angeles Investment Company. *Inexpensive Bungalows: Typical California Homes Costing from $1000 to $2250: designed and built by the Los Angeles Investment Company*. Los Angeles: G. Rice & Sons, 1912.

———. *Practical Bungalows: Typical California Homes, with plans*. Los Angeles: Los Angeles Investment Company, 1912.

McCoy, Esther. *Piecing Together Los Angeles: An Esther McCoy Reader*. Valencia, CA: East of Borneo, in collaboration with the Art School at California Institute of the Arts, 2012.

Ovnick, Merry. "The Mark of Zorro: Silent Film's Impact on 1920s Architecture in Los Angeles." *California History*, Vol. 86, No. 1 (2008): 28–59, 61–64.

Winter, David. *The California Bungalow*. Los Angeles: Hennessey & Ingalls, 1980.

Discover Thousands of Local History Books
Featuring Millions of Vintage Images

Arcadia Publishing, the leading local history publisher in the United States, is committed to making history accessible and meaningful through publishing books that celebrate and preserve the heritage of America's people and places.

Find more books like this at
www.arcadiapublishing.com

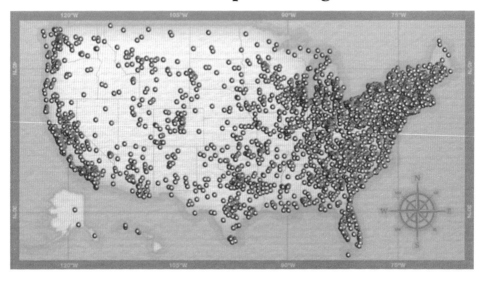

Search for your hometown history, your old stomping grounds, and even your favorite sports team.

Consistent with our mission to preserve history on a local level, this book was printed in South Carolina on American-made paper and manufactured entirely in the United States. Products carrying the accredited Forest Stewardship Council (FSC) label are printed on 100 percent FSC-certified paper.

MADE IN THE USA